The Life of

Bertrand Russell

in pictures and in his own words

Compiled by
Christopher Farley and David Hodgson

First published in 1972 for the Bertrand Russell Centenary
and reprinted in 2004
by Spokesman Books
Russell House, Bulwell Lane, Nottingham NG6 0BT
and printed by the Russell Press Limited (TU)
at the same address

Aged Four

My father, John Russell, afterwards Lord Amberley, was the eldest son of Lord John (afterwards Earl) Russell; my mother, Kate Stanley, was the fourth daughter of Lord Stanley of Alderley.

. . . Both were born in 1842. I have no recollection of my mother, who died when I was two years old, and only very faint recollections of my father, who died twenty months later.

Ravenscroft Then...

My parents married in 1864, when they were both only twenty-two. My brother, as he boasts in his autobiography, was born nine months and four days after the wedding. Shortly before I was born, they went to live in a very lonely house called Ravenscroft (now called Cleddan Hall) in a wood just above the steep banks of the Wye.

. . . And Now

From the house, three days after I was born, my mother wrote a description of me to her mother: "The baby weighed 8¾ lb. is 21 inches long and very fat and very ugly very like Frank everyone thinks, blue eyes far apart and not much chin. He is just like Frank was about nursing. I have lots of milk now, but if he does not get it at once or has wind or anything he gets into such a rage and screams and kicks and trembles till he is soothed off. . . He lifts his head up and looks about in a very energetic way."

 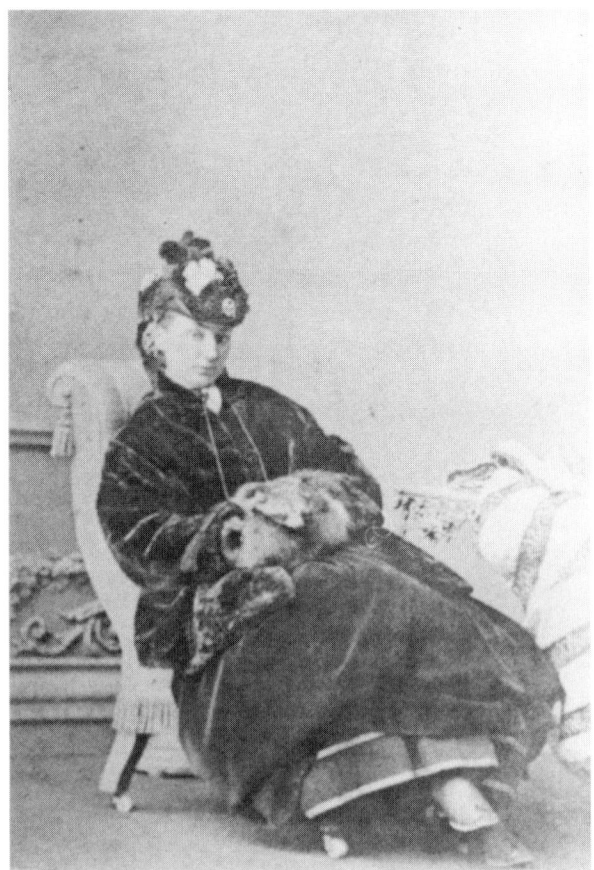

My father was a free-thinker, and wrote a large book, posthumously published, called *An Analysis of Religious Belief*. He had a large library containing the Fathers, works on Buddhism, accounts of Confucianism, and so on. He spent a great deal of time in the country in the preparation of his book.

My mother used to address meetings in favour of votes for women, and I found one passage in her diary where she speaks of the Potter Sisterhood, which included Mrs. Sidney Webb and Lady Courtenay, as social butterflies. Having in later years come to know Mrs. Sidney Webb well, I conceived a considerable respect for my mother's seriousness when I remembered that to her Mrs. Webb seemed frivolous.

The Burial Place at Ravenscroft

In June 1874 my brother fell ill with diptheria, and my mother nursed him back to health; but then my sister Rachel fell ill of the same disease, my mother caught it from her, and both died. My father, who had always been delicate, and had depended upon my mother's vitality, became rapidly more and more of an invalid, and in January 1876 he too died. My brother and I, thenceforth, lived at Pembroke Lodge, with our grandmother Russell, who became a widow in 1878. In a letter of condolence, Queen Victoria wrote: "I trust that your grandsons will grow up all that you could wish." But this comfort was denied to her . . .

My parents had themselves buried in the garden at Ravenscroft, but were dug up and transferred to the family vault at Chenies.

*The death of Bertrand Russell's father, Lord Amberley,
recounted in Maude Stanley's letter to Lady Russell:*

At about 4 a.m. Lizzy (Williams) went into Amberley's room & found him worse but perfectly calm & contented. He looked at her as she came in with a kind & pleasant smile — when she went to his bedside he asked her if she was come to stay with him & she said yes & he said "Stay with me". Then he had chicken broth which he took with pleasure — Lizzy left him for a bit & then came back & was alone with Amberley & Frank who was kneeling on his bed without moving — Amberley asked Lizzy again not to leave him & as she stood close by his bedside he said "Do not go away" — then he said "Help me oh Lizzy help me" & she said "how can I help you?" & he said "pray for me" & then she said some prayers asking God to cast a pitying eye on the bed of affliction & that she trusted God would receive his soul which was near the gate of Heaven — & many other things that came into her mind — Lizzy said "are you happy My Lord" & he said "Yes Lizzy happy, quite happy, & it is long to wait — but it will soon be over with me now" — Lizzy asked him to speak to Frank — he muttered something & said "it is all done" — Frank remained sobbing & crying so that his Father's hand was wet with his tears. The Dr. lifted Bertrand up & he kissed him gently & softly & said "Goodbye my little dears for ever". He then lay perfectly quiet with a smile, never moved or shut his hands, but the breathing at last ceased at 9.30.

Pembroke Lodge in 1883

Pembroke Lodge, where my grandfather and grandmother lived, is a rambling house of only two storeys in Richmond Park. It was in the gift of the Sovereign, and derives its name from the Lady Pembroke to whom George III was devoted in the days of his lunacy. The Queen had given it to my grandparents for their life-time in the 'forties, and they had lived there ever since. The famous Cabinet meeting described in Kinglake's *Invasion of the Crimea,* at which several Cabinet Ministers slept while the Crimean War was decided upon, took place at Pembroke Lodge.

My grandfather, born, like Shelley, in the first month of the first French Republic, was willing to support anti-governmental movements abroad, especially in Italy, though in English affairs, after the passing of the Reform Bill in 1832, he was far from Radical. Nevertheless his principles remained such as would naturally lead to Radicalism in his son, to which he never objected. His pride in my father's bold carrying on of the Russell tradition outweighed their disagreements.

My father's mother was much more radical than Lord John, and after his death developed opinions of which he would hardly have approved, although during his life she had often gently influenced him towards her own views when they differed from his...

When I was a boy, she gave me a Bible with her favourite texts written on the fly-leaf. One of these was "Thou shalt not follow a multitude to do evil." She had a rooted conviction that virtue is only to be found in minorities, and this conviction she transmitted to my father. She had a horror of compromise, and viewed all questions that interested her as simple moral issues, in which the good man had only to obey the voice of conscience. Questions which she could not consider in this way did not interest her.

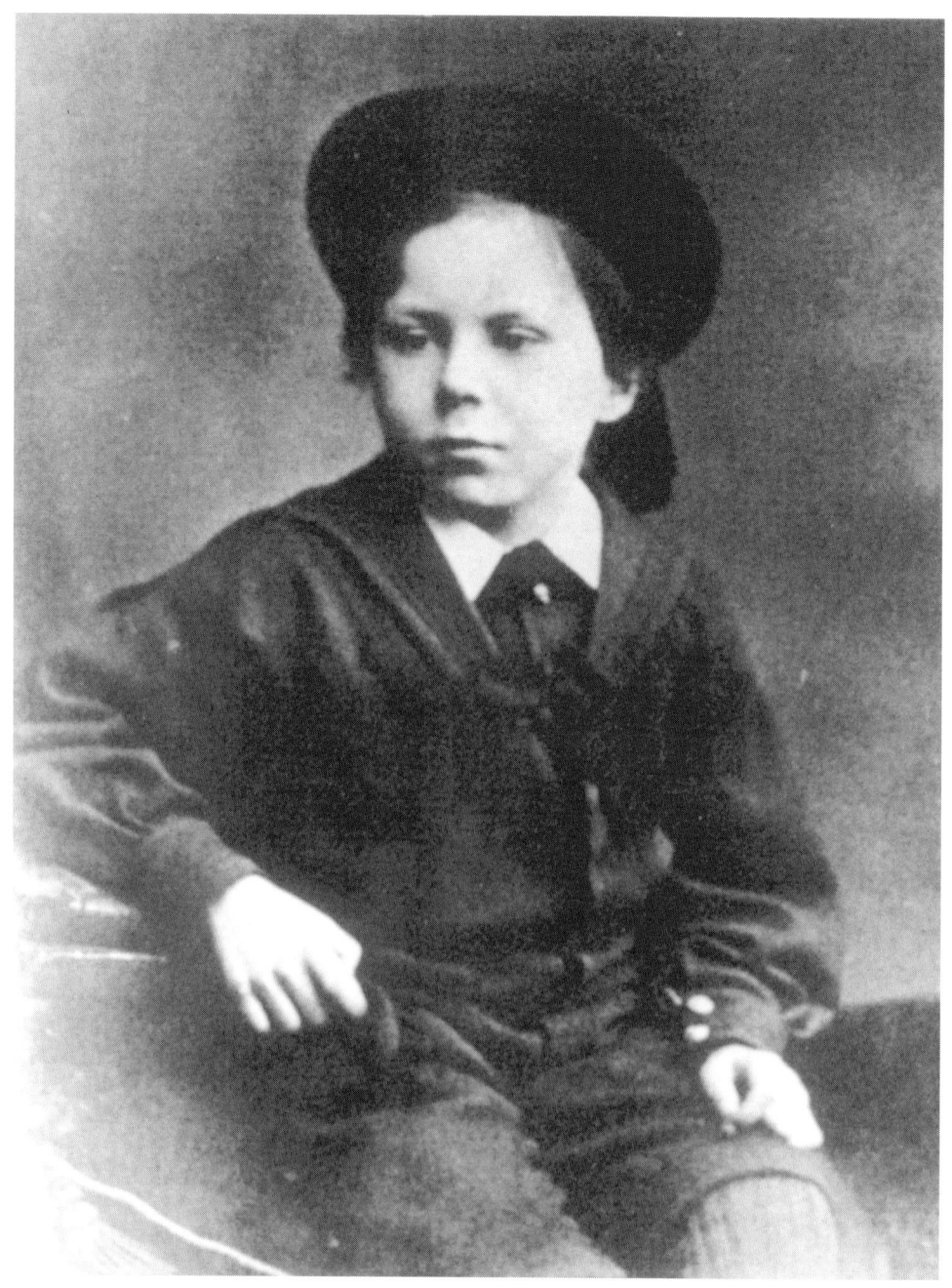

Aged Nine

Pembroke Lodge had eleven acres of garden, mostly allowed to run wild. This garden played a very large part in my life up to the age of eighteen. To the west there was an enormous view extending from the Epsom Downs (which I believed to be the "Ups and Downs") to Windsor Castle, with Hindhead and Leith Hill between. I grew accustomed to wide horizons and to an unimpeded view of the sunset. And I have never since been able to live happily without both. . . Throughout the years during which I lived at Pembroke Lodge, the garden was growing gradually more and more neglected. Big trees fell, shrubs grew over the paths, the grass on the lawns became long and rank, and the box-hedges grew almost into trees. The garden seemed to remember the days of its former splendour, when foreign ambassadors paced its lawns, and princes admired its trim beds of flowers. It lived in the past, and I lived in the past with it.

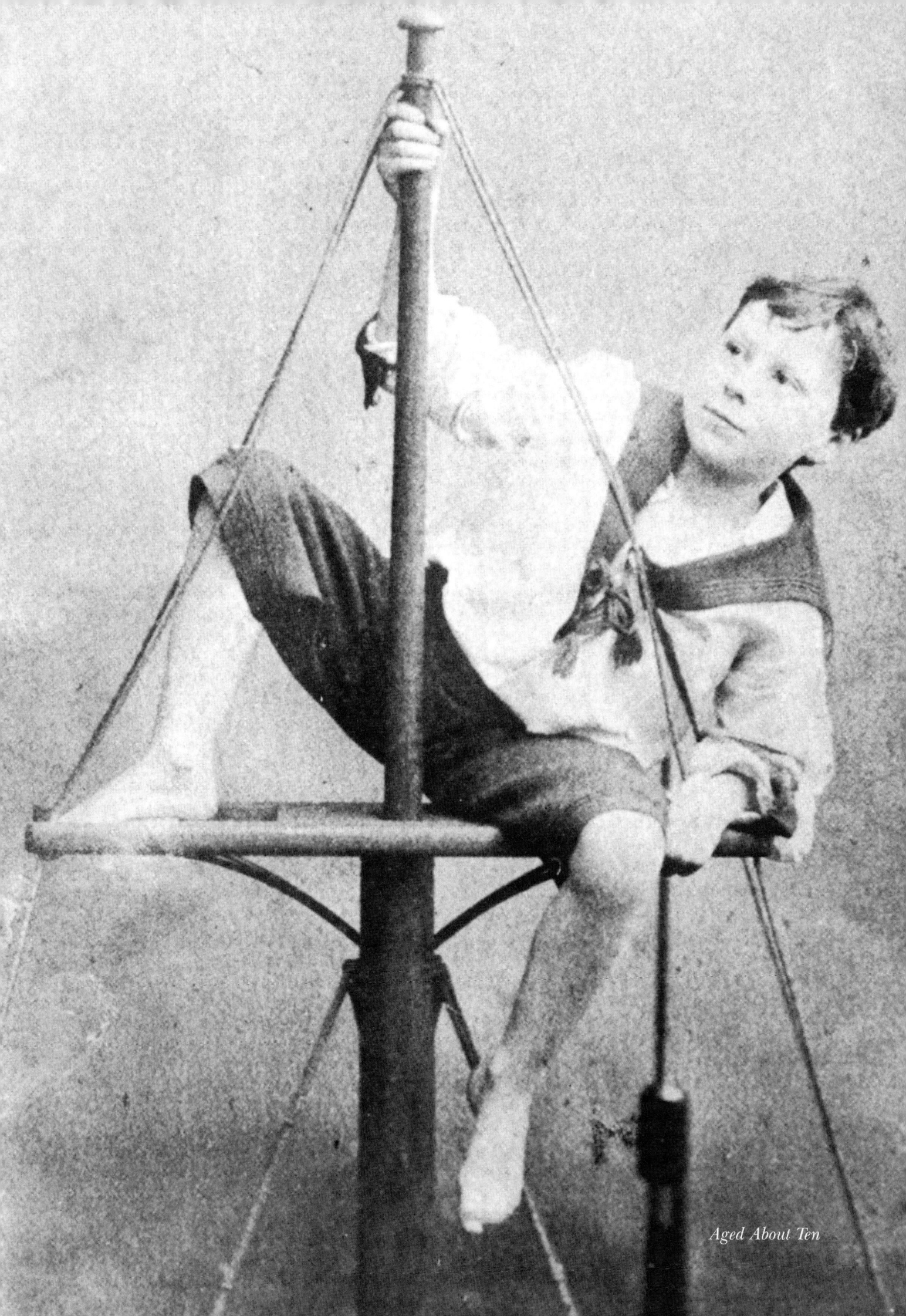

Aged About Ten

My father had been at Cambridge, but my brother was at Oxford. I went to Cambridge because of my interest in mathematics. My first experience of the place was in December 1889 when I was examined for entrance scholarships. I stayed in rooms in the New Court, and I was too shy to enquire the way to the lavatory, so that I walked every morning to the station before the examination began. I saw the Backs through the gate of the New Court, but did not venture to go into them, feeling thay they might be private...

I was very anxious to do well in the scholarship examination, and nervousness somewhat interfered with my work. Nevertheless, I got a minor scholarship, which gave me extreme happiness, as it was the first time I had been able to compare myself with able contemporaries.

From the moment that I went up to Cambridge at the beginning of October 1890 everything went well with me. All the people then in residence who subsequently became my intimate friends called on me during the first week of term. At the time I did not know why they did so, but I discovered afterwards that Whitehead, who had examined for scholarships, had told people to look our for Sanger and me. Sanger was a freshman like myself, also doing mathematics, and also a minor scholar...

As an undergraduate I was persuaded that the Dons were a wholly unnecessary part of the university. I derived no benefits from lectures, and I made a vow to myself that when in due course I became a lecturer I would not suppose that lecturing did any good. I have kept this vow.

I had already been interested in philosophy before I went to Cambridge, but I had not read much except Mill. What I most desired was to find some reason for supposing mathematics true.

The Backs at Trinity College

The greatest happiness of my time at Cambridge was connected with a body whom its members knew as "The Society", but which outsiders, if they knew of it, called "The Apostles". This was a small discussion society, containing one or two people from each year on the average, which met every Saturday night. It has existed since 1820, and has had as members most of the people of any intellectual eminence who have been at Cambridge since then. . . We discussed all manner of things, no doubt with a certain immaturity, but with a detachment and interest scarcely possible in later life. The meetings would generally end about one o'clock at night, and after that I would pace up and down the cloisters of Nevile's Court for hours with one or two other members. We took ourselves perhaps rather seriously, for we considered that the virtue of intellectual honesty was in our keeping. Undoubtedly, we achieved more of this than is common in the world, and I am inclined to think that the best intelligence of Cambridge has been notable in this respect.

Cambridge was important in my life through the fact that it gave me friends, and experience of intellectual discussion, but it was not important through the actual academic instruction. . . Most of what I learned in philosophy has come to seem to me erroneous, and I spent many subsequent years in gradually unlearning the habits of thought which I had there acquired. The one habit of thought of real value that I acquired there was intellectual honesty. This virtue certainly existed not only among my friends, but among my teachers. I cannot remember any instance of a teacher resenting it when one of his pupils showed him to be in error, though I can remember quite a number of occasions on which pupils succeeded in performing this feat. Once during a lecture on hydrostatics, one of the young men interrupted to say: "Have you not forgotten the centrifugal forces on the lid?" The lecturer gasped, and then said: "I have been doing this example that way for twenty years, but you are right". It was a blow to me during the War to find that, even at Cambridge, intellectual honesty had its limitations. Until then, wherever I lived, I felt that Cambridge was the only place on earth that I could regard as home.

*Alys Pearsall Smith
Bertrand Russell's first wife*

She was very beautiful... She was more emanicipated than any young women I had known, since she was at college and crossed the Atlantic alone, and was, as I soon discovered, an intimate friend of Walt Whitman. She asked me whether I had ever read a certain German book called *Ekkehard*, and it happened that I had finished it that morning. I felt this was a stroke of luck. She was kind, and made me feel not shy. I fell in love with her at first sight...

With each year that passed I became more devoted to Alys, the unmarried daughter. She was less flippant than her brother Logan, and less irresponsible than her sister Mrs Costelloe. She seemed to me to possess all the simple kindness which I still cherished in spite of Pembroke Lodge, but to be devoid of priggery and prejudice. I wondered whether she would remain unmarried until I grew up, for she was five years older than I was. It seemed unlikely, but I became increasingly determined that, if she did, I would ask her to marry me...

My people, however, were not at the end of their attempts [to prevent a marriage]. In August they induced Lord Dufferin, who was then our Ambassador in Paris, to offer me the post of honorary attaché. I had no wish to take it, but my grandmother said that she was not much longer for this world, and that I owed it to her to see whether separation would lessen my infatuation. I did not wish to feel remorse whenever she came to die, so I agreed to go to Paris for a minimum of three months, on the understanding that if that produced no effect upon my feelings, my people would no longer actively oppose my marriage. My career in diplomacy, however, was brief and inglorious. I loathed the work, and the people, and the atmosphere of cynicism, and the separation from Alys. My brother came over to visit me, and although I did not know it at the time, he had been asked to come by my people, in order to form a judgment on the situation. He came down strongly on my side, and when the three months were up, which was on November 17th, I shook the dust of Paris off my feet and returned to Alys.

WHY DIDN'T MR. CHAPLIN MIND THE BABY?

when he was President of the Local Government Board from 1895 to 1900.

Overcrowding and Bad Sanitary Conditions caused the

Unnecessary Sacrifice

of

40,000 Infant Lives Every Year!

What did he do for the Protection of Children and the Reduction of Infant Mortality?

If Women had Parliamentary Votes

they would try to alter the

Bad Land Laws

which cause these bad housing conditions and result in such wicked waste of life.

But Mr. Chaplin wants to make the Baby's Food and Clothing Dearer,

and this will only

MAKE MATTERS WORSE.

Therefore

VOTE for RUSSELL

and

And Give Women Votes to Protect the Children.

Printed and Published by A. K. Hollet (T.U.), 110, Haydon's Road, Wimbledon

In 1907 I even stood for Parliament at a by-election, on behalf of votes for women... When, in later years, I campaigned against the first world war, the popular opposition that I encountered was not comparable to that which the suffragists met in 1907. The whole subject was treated, by a great majority of the population, as one for mere hilarity. The crowd would shout derisive remarks: to women, "Go home and mind the baby"; to men, "Does your mother know you're out?" no matter what the man's age. Rotten eggs were aimed at me and hit my wife. At my first meeting rats were let loose to frighten the ladies, and ladies who were in the plot screamed in pretended terror with a view to disgracing their sex.

1902   (20)

Everything, even the object of the book, has been sacrificed to making the proofs look short and neat. It is _essential_, especially in the early parts, that the proofs be written out fully —

[A. N. Whitehead]

[A criticism of my first draft of the Logic of Propositions for the beginning of Principia Mathematica. Whitehead was entirely right.]

Alfred North Whitehead
Collaborator in Principia Mathematica

Every morning I would sit down before a blank sheet of paper. Throughout the day, with a brief interval for lunch, I would stare at the blank sheet. Often when evening came it was still empty. We spent our winters in London, and during the winters I did not attempt to work, but the two summers of 1903 and 1904 remain in my mind as a period of complete intellectual deadlock. It was clear to me that I could not get on without solving the contradictions, and I was determined that no difficulty should turn me aside from the completion of *Principia Mathematica,* but it seemed quite likely that the whole of the rest of my life might be consumed in looking at that blank sheet of paper. . .

The manuscript became more and more vast, and every time that I went out for a walk I used to be afraid that the house would catch fire and the manuscript get burnt up. It was not, of course, the sort of manuscript that could be typed, or even copied. When we finally took it to the University Press, it was so large that we had to hire an old four-wheeler for the purpose. .

So I persisted, and in the end the work was finished, but my intellect never quite recovered from the strain. I have been ever since definitely less capable of dealing with difficult abstractions than I was before.

Although I did not foresee anything like the full disaster of the War, I foresaw a great deal more than most people did. The prospect filled me with horror, but what filled me with even more horror was the fact that the anticipation of carnage was delightful to something like ninety per cent of the population. I had to revise my views on human nature. At that time I was wholly ignorant of psycho-analysis, but I arrived for myself at a view of human passions not unlike that of the psycho-analysts. I arrived at this view in an endeavour to understand popular feeling about the War. I had supposed until that time that it was quite common for parents to love their children, but the War persuaded me that it is a rare exception. I had supposed that most people liked money better than almost anything else, but I discovered that they liked destruction even better. I had supposed that intellectuals frequently loved truth, but I found here again that not ten per cent of them prefer truth to popularity. Gilbert Murray, who had been a close friend of mine since 1902, was a pro-Boer when I was not. I therefore naturally expected that he would again be on the side of peace; yet he went out of his way to write about the wickedness of the Germans, and the super-human virtue of Sir Edward Grey. I became filled with despairing tenderness towards the young men who were to be slaughtered, and with rage against all the statesmen of Europe. For several weeks, I felt that if I should happen to meet Asquith or Grey I should be unable to refrain from murder. Gradually, however, these personal feelings disappeared. They were swallowed up by the magnitude of the tragedy, and by the realization of the popular forces which the statesmen merely let loose.

I was myself tortured by patriotism. The successes of the Germans before the Battle of the Marne were horrible to me. I desired the defeat of Germany as ardently as any retired colonel. Love of England is very nearly the strongest emotion I possess, and in appearing to set it aside at such a moment, I was making a very difficult renunciation. Nevertheless, I never had a moment's doubt as to what I must do. I have at times been paralysed by scepticism, at times I have been cynical, at other times indifferent, but when the War came I felt as if I heard the voice of God. I knew that it was my business to protest, however futile protest might be. My whole nature was involved. As a lover of truth, the national propaganda of all the belligerent nations sickened me. As a lover of civilisation, the return to barbarism appalled me. As a man of thwarted parental feeling, the massacre of the young wrung my heart. I hardly supposed that much good would come of opposing the War, but I felt that for the honour of human nature those who were not swept off their feet should show that they stood firm. After seeing troop trains departing from Waterloo, I used to have strange visions of London as a place of unreality. I used in imagination to see the bridges collapse and sink, and the whole great city vanish like a morning mist. Its inhabitants began to seem like hallucinations, and I would wonder whether the world in which I thought I had lived was a mere product of my own febrile nightmares. Such moods, however, were brief, and were put an end to by the need to work.

Georg Cantor

David Hilbert

Gottlob Frege

Friends and Contemporaries

Joseph Conrad

D.H. Lawrence

Lady Constance Malleson

Lucy Donnelly

Sidney and Beatrice Webb

Stanley Unwin

T.S. Eliot

Harold Laski

J.M. Keynes

George Bernard Shaw

Lady Ottoline Morrell

There was a little weekly newspaper called *The Tribunal,* issued by the No Conscription Fellowship, and I used to write weekly articles for it. After I had ceased to be editor, the new editor, being ill one week, asked me at the last moment to write the weekly article. I did so, and in it I said that American soldiers would be employed as strike-breakers in England, an occupation to which they were accustomed when in their own country. This statement was supported by a Senate Report which I quoted. I was sentenced for this to six months' imprisonment. All this, however, was by no means unpleasant. It kept my self-respect alive, and gave me something to think about less painful than the universal destruction. By the intervention of Arthur Balfour, I was placed in the first division, so that while in prison I was able to read and write as much as I liked, provided I did no pacifist propaganda. I found prison in many ways quite agreeable. I had no engagements, no difficult decisions to make, no fear of callers, no interruptions to my work. I read enormously; I wrote a book, *Introduction to Mathematical Philosophy,* a semi-popular version of *The Principles of Mathematics,* and began the work for *Analysis of Mind.* I was rather interested in my fellow-prisoners, who seemed to me in no way morally inferior to the rest of the population, though they were on the whole slightly below the usual level of intelligence, as was shown by their having been caught. For anybody not in the first division, especially for a person accustomed to reading and writing, prison is a severe and terrible punishment; but for me, thanks to Arthur Balfour, this was not so. I owe him gratitude for his intervention although I was bitterly opposed to all his policies. I was much cheered, on my arrival, by the warder at the gate, who had to take particulars about me. He asked my religion and I replied "agnostic". He asked how to spell it, and remarked with a sigh: "Well, there are many religions, but I suppose they all worship the same God". This remark kept me cheerful for about a week. One time, when I was reading Strachey's *Eminent Victorians,* I laughed so loud that the warder came round to stop me, saying I must remember that prison was a place of punishment.

At eleven o'clock, when the Armistice was announced, I was in Tottenham Court Road. Within two minutes everybody in all the shops and offices had come into the street. They commandeered the buses, and made them go where they liked. I saw a man and woman, complete strangers to each other, meet in the middle of the road and kiss as they passed.

Late into the night I stayed alone in the streets, watching the temper of the crowd, as I had done in the August days four years before. The crowd was frivolous still, and had learned nothing during the period of horror, except to snatch at pleasure more recklessly than before. I felt strangely solitary amid the rejoicings, like a ghost dropped by accident from some other planet. True, I rejoiced also, but I could find nothing in common between my rejoicing and that of the crowd. Throughout my life I have longed to feel that oneness with large bodies of human beings that is experienced by the members of enthusiastic crowds. The longing has often been strong enough to lead me into self-deception. I have imagined myself in turn a Liberal, a Socialist, or a Pacifist, but I have never been any of these things, in any profound sense. Always the sceptical intellect, when I have most wished it silent, has whispered doubts to me, has cut me off from the facile enthusiasms of others, and has transported me into a desolate solitude. During the War, while I worked with Quakers, non-resisters, and socialists, while I was willing to accept the unpopularity and the inconvenience belonging to unpopular opinions, I would tell the Quakers that I thought many wars in history had been justified, and the socialists that I dreaded the tyranny of the State. They would look askance at me, and while continuing to accept my help would feel that I was not one of them. Underlying all occupations and all pleasures I have felt since early youth the pain of solitude.

The War of 1914-18 changed everything for me. I ceased to be academic and took to writing a new kind of books. I changed my whole conception of human nature. I became for the first time deeply convinced that Puritanism does not make for human happiness. Through the spectacle of death I acquired a new love for what is living. I became convinced that most human beings are possessed by a profound unhappiness venting itself in destructive rages, and that only through the diffusion of instinctive joy can a good world be brought into being. I saw that reformers and reactionaries alike in our present world have become distorted by cruelties. I grew suspicious of all purposes demanding stern discipline. Being in opposition to the whole purpose of the community, and finding all the everyday virtues used as means for the slaughter of Germans, I experienced great difficulty in not becoming a complete Antinomian. But I was saved from this by the profound compassion which I felt for the sorrows of the world.

A Labour deputation was going to Russia [in 1920], and was willing that I should accompany it. The Government considered my application, and after causing me to be interviewed by H.A.L. Fisher, they decided to let me go. The Soviet Government was more difficult to persuade, and when I was already in Stockholm on the way, Litvinov was still refusing permission, in spite of our having been fellow prisoners in Brixton. However, the objections of the Soviet Government were at last overcome. . .

By far the most important aspect of the Russian Revolution is as an attempt to realise Socialism. I believe that Socialism is necessary to the world, and believe that the heroism of Russia has fired men's hopes in a way which was essential to the realisation of Socialism in the future. Regarded as a splendid attempt, without which ultimate success would have been very improbable, Bolshevism deserves the gratitude and admiration of all the progressive part of mankind.

But the method by which Moscow aims at establishing Socialism is a pioneer method, rough and dangerous, too heroic to count the cost of the opposition it arouses. I do not believe that by this method a stable or desirable form of Socialism can be established.

*Dora Black
Bertrand Russell's second wife*

Those who have known her only in her public capacity would scarcely credit the quality of elfin charm which she possessed whenever the sense of responsibility did not weigh her down. Bathing by moonlight, or running with bare feet on the dewy grass, she won my imagination as completely as on her serious side she appealed to my desire for parenthood and my sense of social responsibility.

The National University of Peking for which I lectured [1920-21] was a very remarkable institution. The Chancellor and the Vice-Chancellor were men passionately devoted to the modernizing of China. The Vice-Chancellor was one of the most whole-hearted idealists that I have ever known. The funds which should have gone to pay salaries were always being appropriated by Tuchuns, so that the teaching was mainly a labour of love. The students deserved what their professors had to give them. They were ardently desirous of knowledge, and there was no limit to the sacrifices that they were prepared to make for their country. The atmosphere was electric with the hope of a great awakening. After centuries of slumber, China was becoming aware of the modern world, and at that time the sordidness and compromises that go with governmental responsibility had not yet descended upon the reformers. The English sneered at the reformers, and said that China would always be China. They assured me that it was silly to listen to the frothy talk of half-baked young men; yet within a few years those half-baked young men had conquered China and deprived the English of many of their most cherished privileges.

VOTE
for
RUSSELL
....
LABOUR
CANDIDATE

I also stood for Parliament in Chelsea in 1922 and 1923, and Dora stood in 1924.

Ever since the day, in the summer of 1894, when I walked with Alys on Richmond Green. . . I had tried to suppress my desire for children. It had, however, grown continually stronger, until it had become almost insupportable. When my first child was born, in November 1921, I felt an immense release of pent-up emotion, and during the next ten years my main purposes were parental. Parental feeling, as I have experienced it, is very complex. There is, first and foremost, sheer animal affection, and delight in watching what is charming in the ways of the young. Next, there is the sense of inescapable responsibility, providing a purpose for daily activities which scepticism does not easily question. Then there is an egoistic element, which is very dangerous: the hope that one's children may succeed where one has failed, that they may carry on one's work when death or senility puts an end to one's own efforts, and, in any case, that they will supply a biological escape from death, making one's own life part of the whole stream, and not a mere stagnant puddle without any overflow into the future. All this I experienced, and for some years it filled my life with happiness and peace.

My brother died suddenly in Marseilles. I inherit from him a title, but not a penny of money, as he was a bankrupt. A title is a great nuisance to me, and I am at a loss what to do, but at any rate I do not wish it employed in connection with any of my literary work. There is, so far as I know, only one method of getting rid of it, which is to be attainted of high treason, and this would involve my head being cut off on Tower Hill. This method seems to me perhaps somewhat extreme.

In 1927, Dora and I came to a decision, for which we were equally responsible, to found a school of our own in order that our children might be educated as we thought best. We believed, perhaps mistakenly, that children need the companionship of a group of other children, and that, therefore, we ought no longer to be content to bring up our children without others. But we did not know of any existing school that seemed to us in any way satisfactory. We wanted an unusual combination: on the one hand, we disliked prudery and religious instruction and a great many restraints on freedom which are taken for granted in conventional schools; on the other hand, we could not agree with most 'modern' educationists in thinking scholastic instruction unimportant, or in advocating a *complete* absence of discipline. We therefore endeavoured to collect a group of about twenty children, of roughly the same ages as John and Kate, with a view to keeping these same children throughout their school years.

For the purposes of the school we rented my brother's house, Telegraph House, on the South Downs, between Chichester and Petersfield. This owed its name to having been a semaphore station in the time of George III, one of a string of such stations by which messages were flashed between Portsmouth and London. Probably the news of Trafalgar reached London in this way.

The original house was quite small, but my brother gradually added to it. He was passionately devoted to the place, and wrote about it at length in his autobiography, which he called *My Life and Adventures*. The house was ugly and rather absurd, but the situation was superb. There were enormous views to East and South and West; in one direction one saw over the Sussex Weald to Leith Hill, in another one saw the Isle of Wight and the liners approaching Southampton. There was a tower with large windows on all four sides. Here I made my study, and I have never known one with a more beautiful outlook.

Four characteristics seem to me jointly to form the basis of an ideal character: vitality, courage, sensitiveness, and intelligence. I do not suggest that this list is complete, but I think it carries us a good way. Moreover, I firmly believe that, by proper physical, emotional and intellectual care of the young, these qualities could all be made very common.

In managing the school we experienced a number of difficulties which we ought to have foreseen. There was, first, the problem of finance. It became obvious that there must be an enormous pecuniary loss. We could only have prevented this by making the school large and the food inadequate, and we could not make the school large except by altering its character so as to appeal to conventional parents. Fortunately I was at this time making a great deal of money from books and from lecture tours in America. I made four such tours altogether — during 1924. . . 1927, 1929 and 1931. The one in 1927 was during the first term of the school, so that I had no part in its beginnings. During the second term, Dora went on a lecture tour in America. Thus throughout the first two terms there was never more than one of us in charge. When I was not in America, I had to write books to make the necessary money. Consequently, I was never able to give my whole time to the school.

A second difficulty was that some of the staff, however often and however meticulously our principles were explained to them, could never be brought to act in accordance with them unless one of us was present.

A third trouble, and that perhaps the most serious, was that we got an undue proportion of problem children. We ought to have been on the look-out for this pit-fall, but at first we were glad to take almost any child. The parents who were most inclined to try new methods were those who had difficulties with their children. As a rule, these difficulties were the fault of the parents, and the ill effects of their unwisdom were renewed in each holiday. Whatever may have been the cause, many of the children were cruel and destructive. To let the children go free was to establish a reign of terror, in which the strong kept the weak trembling and miserable. A school is like the world: only government can prevent brutal violence. And so I found myself, when the children were not at lessons, obliged to supervise them continually to stop cruelty. We divided them into three groups, bigs, middles, and smalls. One of the middles was perpetually ill-treating the smalls, so I asked him why he did it. His answer was: "The bigs hit me, so I hit the smalls: that's fair". And he really thought it was.

In 1936, I married Peter Spence and my youngest child, Conrad,
was born in 1937. This was a great happiness.

Bertrand and Patricia Russell, with Conrad, Kate and John in 1940

Towards the end of the academic year 1939-40, I was invited to become a professor at the College of the City of New York...

A lady, whose daughter attended some section of the City College with which I should never be brought in contact, was induced to bring a suit, saying that my presence in that institution would be dangerous to her daughter's virtue. This was not a suit against me, but against the Municipality of New York. I endeavoured to be made a party to the suit, but was told that I was not concerned. Although the Municipality was nominally the defendant, it was as anxious to lose the suit as the good lady was to win it. The lawyer for the prosecution pronounced my works "lecherous, libidinous, lustful, venerous, erotomaniac, aphrodisiac, irreverent, narrow-minded, untruthful, and bereft of moral fiber". The suit came before an Irishman who decided against me at length and with vituperation...

A typical American witch-hunt was instituted against me, and I became taboo throughout the whole of the United States.

C.C.N.Y. STUDENTS APPROVE RUSSELL AT RALLY
NEW YORK CITY — A GENERAL VIEW IN GREAT HALL
AS SOME 2,500 STUDENTS OF THE CITY COLLEGE OF
NEW YORK HELD A RALLY HERE APRIL 5TH TO VOICE
THEIR APPROVAL OF BERTRAND RUSSELL AND TO PROTEST
THE REVOCATION OF THE BRITISH PHILOSOPHER'S
APPOINTMENT TO THE FACULTY.
CREDIT LINE (ACME) NY CHI LA CL   4—5—40 (JO)

During the year 1944, it became gradually clear that the war was ending, and was ending in German defeat. This made it possible for us to return to England and to bring our children with us without serious risk...

Trinity College had invited me to a five-year lectureship and I had accepted the invitation. It carried with it a fellowship and a right to rooms in College. I went to Cambridge and found that the rooms were altogether delightful; they looked out on the bowling green, which was a mass of flowers. It was a relief to find that the beauty of Cambridge was undimmed, and I found the peacefulness of the Great Court almost unbelievably soothing.

But the problem of housing Peter and Conrad remained. Cambridge was incredibly full, and at first the best that I could achieve was squalid rooms in a lodging house. There they were underfed and miserable, while I was living luxuriously in College. As soon as it became clear that I was going to get money. . . I bought a house in Cambridge, where we lived for some time.

VJ-day and the General Election which immediately followed it occurred while we were living in this house. It was also there that I wrote most of my book on *Human Knowledge, its Scope and Limits*. I could have been happy in Cambridge, but the Cambridge ladies did not consider us respectable.

In 1945

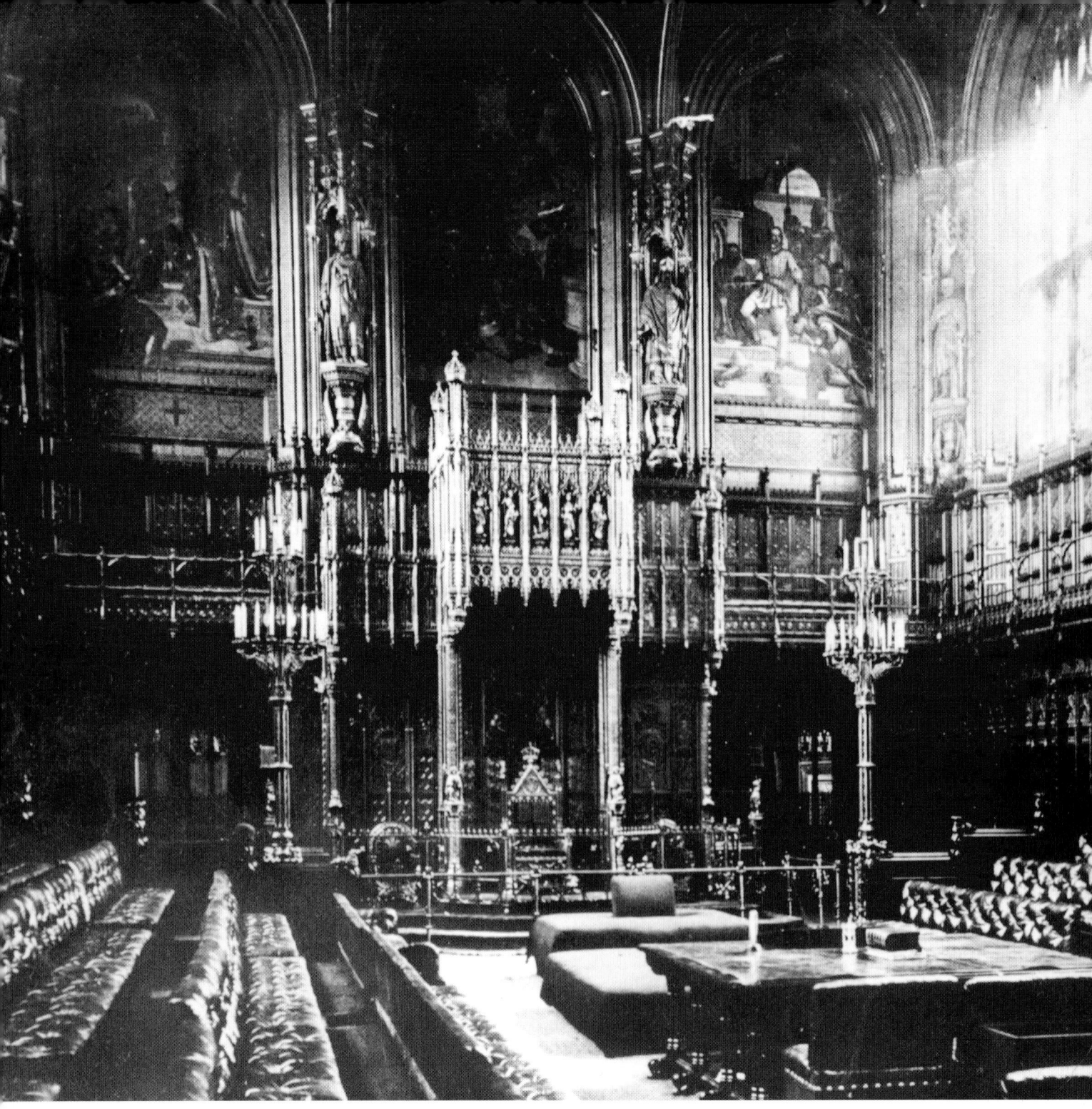

The bombing of Hiroshima and Nagasaki in 1945 first brought the possibility of nuclear war to the attention of men of science and even of some few politicians. A few months after the bombing of the two Japanese cities, I made a speech in the House of Lords pointing out the likelihood of a general nuclear war and the certainty of its causing universal disaster if it occurred. I forecast and explained the making of nuclear bombs of far greater power than those used upon Hiroshima and Nagasaki, fusion as against the old fission bombs, the present hydrogen bombs in fact... Everybody applauded my speech; not a single Peer suggested that my fears were excessive. But all my hearers agreed that this was a question for their grandchildren...

Those who try to make you uneasy by talk about atom bombs are regarded as trouble-makers, as people to be avoided, as people who spoil the pleasure of a fine day by foolish prospects of improbable rain.

I bought a small house at Ffestiniog in North Wales with a most lovely view.

Some years before I gave the Reith Lectures, my old professor and friend and collaborator in *Principia Mathematica*, A.N. Whitehead, had been given the OM. Now, by the early part of 1950, I had become so respectable in the eyes of the Establishment that it was felt that I, too, should be given the OM. This made me very happy for, though I daresay it would surprise many Englishmen and most of the English Establishment to hear it, I am passionately English, and I treasure an honour bestowed on me by the Head of my country. I had to go to Buckingham Palace for the official bestowal of it. The King was affable, but somewhat embarrassed at having to behave graciously to so queer a fellow, a convict to boot. He remarked, "You have sometimes behaved in a way which would not do if generally adopted". I have been glad ever since that I did not make the reply that sprang to my mind: "Like your brother." But he was thinking of things like my having been a conscientious objector, and I did not feel that I could let this remark pass in silence, so I said: "How a man should behave depends upon his profession. A postman, for instance, should knock at all the doors in a street at which he has letters to deliver, but if anybody else knocked on all the doors, he would be considered a public nuisance." The King, to avoid answering, abruptly changed the subject...

I went again to the United States. I had been asked to "give a short course" in philosophy for a month at Mt Holyoak College, a well-known college for women in New England. From there I went to Princeton where I, as usual, delivered a lecture and again met various old friends, among them Einstein. There I received the news that I was to be given a Nobel Prize.

When I was called to Stockholm, at the end of 1950, to receive the Nobel Prize — somewhat to my surprise, for literature, for my book *Marriage and Morals* —I was apprehensive...

1950, beginning with the OM and ending with the Nobel Prize, seems to have marked the apogee of my respectability. It is true that I began to feel slightly uneasy, fearing that this might mean the onset of blind orthodoxy. I have always held that no one can be respectable without being wicked, but so blunted was my moral sense that I could not see in what way I had sinned.

Bertrand Russell's own caption to this photograph:

> I think I could turn and live with animals, they are so placid
>   and self-contained,
> I stand and look at them long and long.
> They do not sweat and whine about their condition,
> They do not lie awake in the dark and weep for their sins,
> They do not make me sick discussing their duty to God,
> Not one is dissatisfied, not one is demented with the mania of
>   owning things,
> Not one kneels to another, nor to his kind that lived thousands
>   of years ago,
> Not one is respectable or unhappy over the whole earth.
>
> *Walt Whitman*

At the end of June, 1950, I went to Australia in response to an invitation by the Australian Institute of International Affairs to give lectures at various universities on subjects connected with the Cold War. I interpreted this subject liberally and my lectures dealt with speculation about the future of industrialism.

To Edith

Through the long years
    I sought peace.
I found ecstasy, I found anguish,
    I found madness,
    I found loneliness.
I found the solitary pain
    that gnaws the heart,
But peace I did not find.

Now, old & near my end,
    I have known you,
And, knowing you,
I have found both ecstasy & peace,
    I know rest.
After so many lonely years.
I know what life & love may be.
Now, if I sleep,
    I shall sleep fulfilled.

Edith Finch
Bertrand Russell's fourth wife

It had occurred to me that it might be possible to formulate a statement that a number of very well-known and respected scientists of both capitalist and communist ideologies would be willing to sign calling for further joint action. Before taking any measures, however, I had written to Einstein to learn what he thought of such a plan. He had replied with enthusiasm, but had said that, because he was not well and could hardly keep up with present commitments, he himself could do nothing to help beyond sending me the names of various scientists who, he thought, would be sympathetic. He had begged me, nevertheless, to carry out my idea and to formulate the statement myself. This I had done, basing the statement upon my Christmas broadcast, "Man's Peril".

With Vanessa Redgrave

With Professor Josef Rotblat

With U Thant

With Dr. Albert Schweitzer

Plas Penrhyn... was small and unpretentious, but had a delightful garden and little orchard and a number of fine beech trees. Above all, it had a most lovely view, south to the sea, west to Portmadoc and the Caernarvon hills, and north up the valley of the Glaslyn to Snowdon. I was captivated by it, and particularly pleased that across the valley could be seen the house where Shelley had lived. The owner of Plas Penrhyn agreed to let it to us largely, I think, because he, too, is a lover of Shelley.

My cousin Maud Russell invited us to a party celebrating the achievement of the mosaic floor designed by Boris Anrep in the National Gallery. My portrait summoning Truth from a well occurs there with portraits of some of my contemporaries.

"There lies before us, if we choose, continual progress in happiness, knowledge, and wisdom. Shall we, instead, choose death, because we cannot forget our quarrels? I appeal, as a human being to human beings: remember your humanity, and forget the rest. If you can do so, the way lies open to a new Paradise; if you cannot, nothing lies before you but universal death."

"Ladies and gentlemen, the purpose of this conference is to bring to your notice, and through you to the notice of the world, a statement signed by eight of the most eminent scientists in the field cognate to nuclear warfare, about the perils that are involved in nuclear warfare and the absolute necessity therefore of avoiding war. .."

July 1955

September 1961

"We are appealing for support for a movement of non-violent resistance to nuclear war and weapons of mass extermination. Our appeal is made from a common consciousness of the appalling peril to which Governments of East and West are exposing the human race."

"If the Court permits, I should like to make a short statement as to the reasons for my present course. This is my personal statement, but I hope that those who are accused of the same so-called crime will be in sympathy with what I have to say.

It was only step by step and with great reluctance that we were driven to non-violent civil disobedience.

Ever since the bomb was dropped on Hiroshima on August 6th, 1945, I have been profoundly troubled by the danger of nuclear warfare. I began my attempt to warn people by entirely orthodox methods. .''

COMMITTEE OF 100
ACTION FOR LIFE

1962

"You, your families, your friends and your countries are to be exterminated by the common decision of a few brutal but powerful men. To please these men, all the private affections, all the public hopes, all that has been achieved in art, and knowledge and thought and all that might be achieved hereafter is to be wiped out forever.

Our ruined lifeless planet will continue for countless ages to circle aimlessly round the sun unredeemed by the joys and loves, the occasional wisdom and the power to create beauty which have given value to human life.

It is for seeking to prevent this that we are in prison."

90th Birthday Medallion by Christopher Ironside

Plas Penrhyn

Rather against my will my colleagues urged that the Bertrand Russell Peace Foundation should bear my name. I knew that this would prejudice against the Foundation many people who might uphold our work itself. . . My colleagues contended that, as I had been carrying on the work for years, helped by them during the last few years, and my name was identified with it in many parts of the world, to omit my name would mean a set-back for the work. I was pleased by their determination, though still somewhat dubious of its wisdom. But in the end I agreed.

View from Bertrand Russell's bedroom at Plas Penrhyn

I have given countless newspaper and TV interviews and made several films. The general rule to which I adhere in determining to which requests for interviews to accede to is to refuse all those that show signs of being concerned with details of what is known as my "private life" rather than my work and ideas. The latter, I am glad to have publicized, and I welcome honest reports and criticisms of them.

Lord Russell

All earthly knowledge finally explored,
  Man feels himself from doubt and dogma free.
There are more things in Heaven, though, my lord,
  Than are dreamed of in your philosophy.

There are more things in
heaven & earth, Horatio,
than are dreamt of in your
philosophy.

On the contrary: put
$$\omega = \hat{x}(x \sim \varepsilon x)$$
Then
$$\omega \sim \varepsilon \omega \equiv \omega \varepsilon \omega$$
I dreamt of ω, but it
wasn't in heaven or earth

Some classes are members
of themselves, some are not:
the class of all classes is a
class, the class of not-teapots
is a not-teapot.

Consider the class of all
the classes not members of
themselves; if it is a member
of itself, it is not a member
of itself; if it is not, it is.

Bertrand Russell

Principles of Mathematics, p. 102

In the summer of 1966, after extensive study and planning, I wrote to a number of people around the world, inviting them to join an International War Crimes Tribunal. The response heartened me, and soon I had received about eighteen acceptances...

I invited all the members to London for preliminary discussions in November, 1966, and opened the proceedings with a speech... It seemed to me essential that what was happening in Vietnam should be examined with scrupulous care, and I had invited only people whose integrity was beyond question.

I do not know whether my last words should be:

> The bright day is done
> And we are for the dark,

or, as I sometimes allow myself to hope,

> The world's great age begins anew,
> The golden years return . . .
> Heaven smiles, and faith and empires gleam,
> Like wrecks of a dissolving dream.

I have done what I could to add my small weight in an attempt to tip the balance on the side of hope, but it has been a puny effort against vast forces.

May others succeed where my generation failed.

Some old people are oppressed by the fear of death. In the young there is a justification for this feeling. Young men who have reason to fear that they will be killed in battle may justifiably feel bitter in the thought that they have been cheated of the best things that life has to offer. But in an old man who has known human joys and sorrows, and has achieved whatever work it was in him to do, the fear of death is somewhat abject and ignoble. The best way to overcome it — so at least it seems to me — is to make your interests gradually wider and more impersonal, until bit by bit the walls of the ego recede, and your life becomes increasingly merged in the universal life. An individual human existence should be like a river — small at first, narrowly contained within its banks, and rushing passionately past boulders and over waterfalls. Gradually the river grows wider, the banks recede, the waters flow more quietly, and in the end, without any visible break, they become merged in the sea, and painlessly lose their individual being. The man who, in old age, can see his life in this way, will not suffer from the fear of death, since the things he cares for will continue. And if, with the decay of vitality, weariness increases, the thought of rest will not be unwelcome. The wise man should wish to die while still at work, knowing that others will carry on what he can no longer do, and content in the thought that what was possible has been done.

The third Earl Russell, O.M., Fellow of this College, won fame as a writer on, and interpreter of, philosophy, and most particularly the philosophy of mathematics. Long moved by the cruelty of man to man, he gave as an old man with youthful vigour all his powers to the cause of peace between the nations until at last, the bearer of many honours and esteemed the whole world over, he found rest from his labours in 1970, in his 98th year.

Bertrand Russell's Books

GERMAN SOCIAL DEMOCRACY 1896
AN ESSAY ON THE FOUNDATIONS OF GEOMETRY 1897
THE PHILOSOPHY OF LEIBNIZ 1900
THE PRINCIPLES OF MATHEMATICS 1903
PHILOSOPHICAL ESSAYS 1910
PROBLEMS OF PHILOSOPHY 1912
PRINCIPIA MATHEMATICA (with A.N. WHITEHEAD)—Vol. I 1910; Vol. II 1911; Vol. III 1913
OUR KNOWLEDGE OF THE EXTERNAL WORLD 1914
JUSTICE IN WARTIME 1916
PRINCIPLES OF SOCIAL RECONSTRUCTION 1916
POLITICAL IDEALS 1917
ROADS TO FREEDOM 1918
MYSTICISM AND LOGIC 1918
INTRODUCTION TO MATHEMATICAL PHILOSOPHY 1919
THE PRACTICE AND THEORY OF BOLSHEVISM 1920
THE ANALYSIS OF MIND 1921
THE PROBLEM OF CHINA 1922
PROSPECTS OF INDUSTRIAL CIVILISATION (with DORA RUSSELL) 1923
THE ABC OF ATOMS 1923
ICARUS OR THE FUTURE OF SCIENCE 1924
THE ABC OF RELATIVITY 1925
WHAT I BELIEVE 1925
ON EDUCATION 1926
SELECTED PAPERS OF BERTRAND RUSSELL 1927
AN OUTLINE OF PHILOSOPHY 1927
THE ANALYSIS OF MATTER 1927
SCEPTICAL ESSAYS 1928
MARRIAGE AND MORALS 1929
THE CONQUEST OF HAPPINESS 1930
THE SCIENTIFIC OUTLOOK 1931
EDUCATION AND THE SOCIAL ORDER 1932
FREEDOM AND ORGANISATION 1814-1914 1934
IN PRAISE OF IDLENESS 1935
RELIGION AND SCIENCE 1935
WHICH WAY TO PEACE? 1936
THE AMBERLEY PAPERS (with PATRICIA RUSSELL) 1937
POWER 1938
AN INQUIRY INTO MEANING AND TRUTH 1940
HISTORY OF WESTERN PHILOSOPHY 1945
HUMAN KNOWLEDGE: ITS SCOPE AND LIMITS 1948
AUTHORITY AND THE INDIVIDUAL 1949
UNPOPULAR ESSAYS 1950
NEW HOPES FOR A CHANGING WORLD 1951
THE WIT AND WISDOM OF BERTRAND RUSSELL (ed. L. DENONN) 1951
THE IMPACT OF SCIENCE ON SOCIETY 1952
DICTIONARY OF MIND, MATTER AND MORALS (ed. L. DENONN) 1952
THE GOOD CITIZEN'S ALPHABET 1953
SATAN IN THE SUBURBS 1953
NIGHTMARES OF EMINENT PERSONS 1954
HUMAN SOCIETY IN ETHICS AND POLITICS 1954
LOGIC AND KNOWLEDGE (ed. R.C. MARSH) 1956
PORTRAITS FROM MEMORY 1956
UNDERSTANDING HISTORY 1957
WHY I AM NOT A CHRISTIAN (ed. P. EDWARDS) 1957
VITAL LETTERS OF RUSSELL, KRUSHCHEV, DULLES 1958
BERTRAND RUSSELL'S BEST (ed. R. EGNER) 1958
COMMON SENSE AND NUCLEAR WARFARE 1959
MY PHILOSOPHICAL DEVELOPMENT 1959
WISDOM OF THE WEST (ed. P. FOULKES) 1959
BERTRAND RUSSELL SPEAKS HIS MIND 1960
FACT AND FICTION 1961
HAS MAN A FUTURE? 1961
THE BASIC WRITINGS OF BERTRAND RUSSELL (ed. R. EGNER and L. DENONN) 1961
UNARMED VICTORY 1963
ON THE PHILOSOPHY OF SCIENCE (ed. C. FRITZ) 1965
WAR CRIMES IN VIETNAM 1967
THE ART OF PHILOSOPHISING 1968
AUTOBIOGRAPHY — VOL.I 1967; VOL. II 1968; VOL. III 1969
DEAR BERTRAND RUSSELL (ed. B. FEINBERG and R. KASRILS) 1969
THE COLLECTED STORIES OF BERTRAND RUSSELL (ed. B. FEINBERG) 1972

Acknowledgements

David Hodgson is the picture editor of this book, and his own pictures appear on pages 9, 12, 19, 20, 21, 46, 59, 70, 80-81, 83, 92 and 94.

We wish to thank the following for helping to make this book possible:

For the cover portrait we are indebted to Lotte Meitner-Graf of London, whose portraits appear also on pages 65 and 85.

Ara Guler, whose pictures appear on page 84.

The National Portrait Gallery, London, for the picture on page 15.

The National Gallery, London, for the picture on page 71.

Punch, for the cartoon on page 88.

The *New York Post* for the cartoon on page 53.

The Library of Trinity College, Cambridge, for the drawing on page 29.

Other pictures are from Features International, Keystone, Radio Times Hulton, P.A. Pictures, United Press International and the Bertrand Russell Peace Foundation.

We wish to thank George Allen & Unwin Ltd. of London, Bertrand Russell's principal publishers, for permission to reproduce extracts from his books.